LINEN

&

STONE

notes

notes

notes

notes

notes

notes

notes

notes

notes

notes

notes

notes

notes

planner

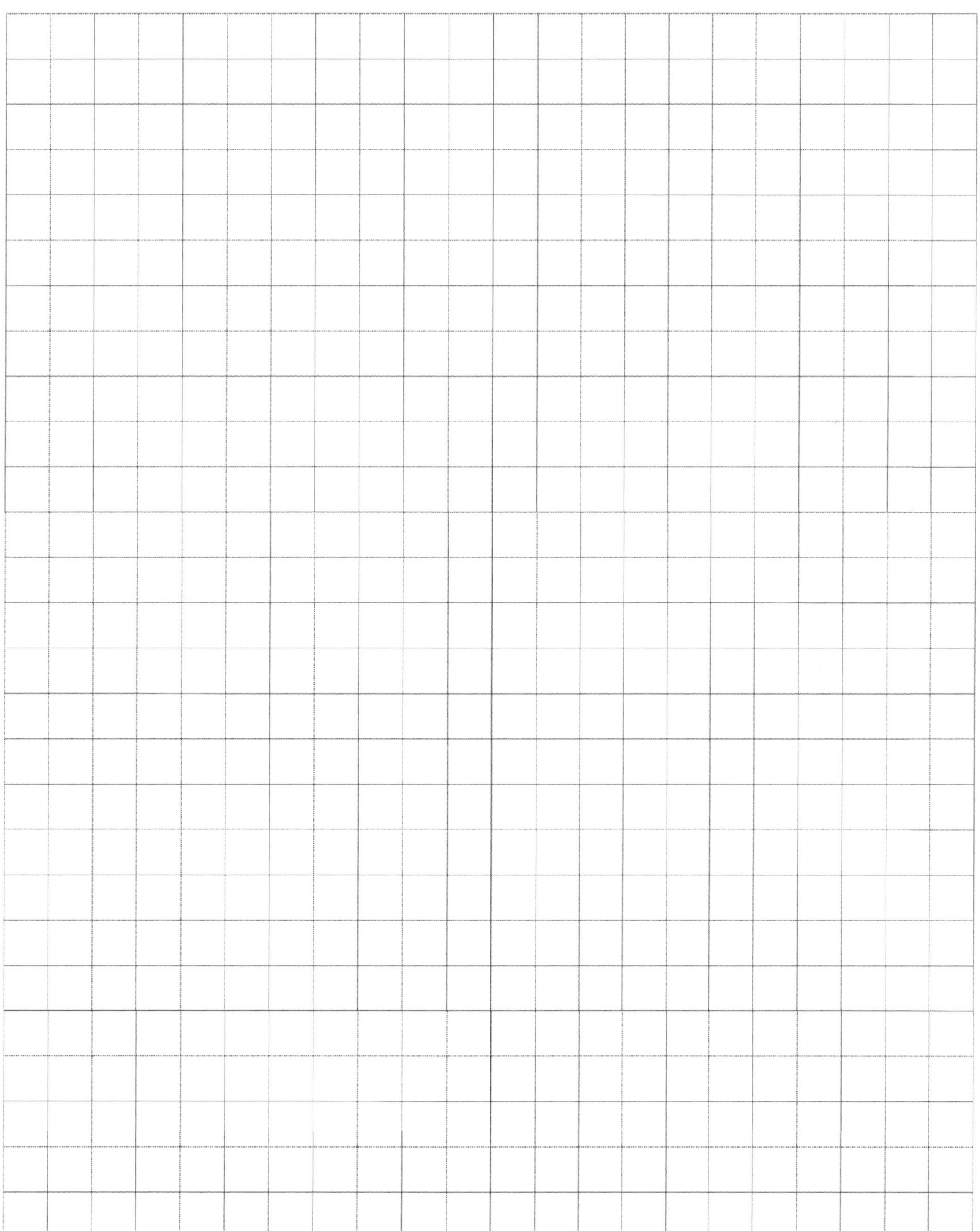

planner

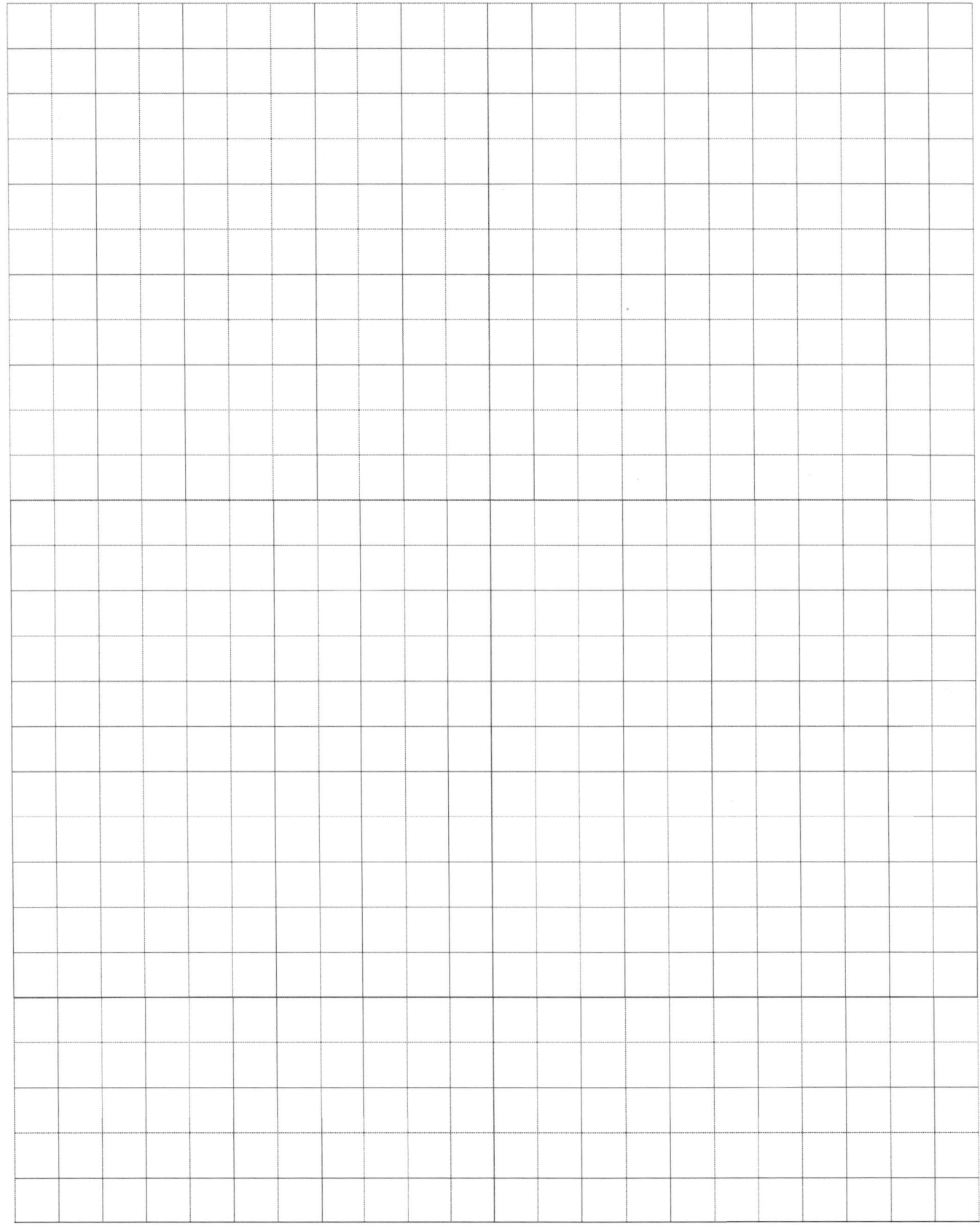

planner

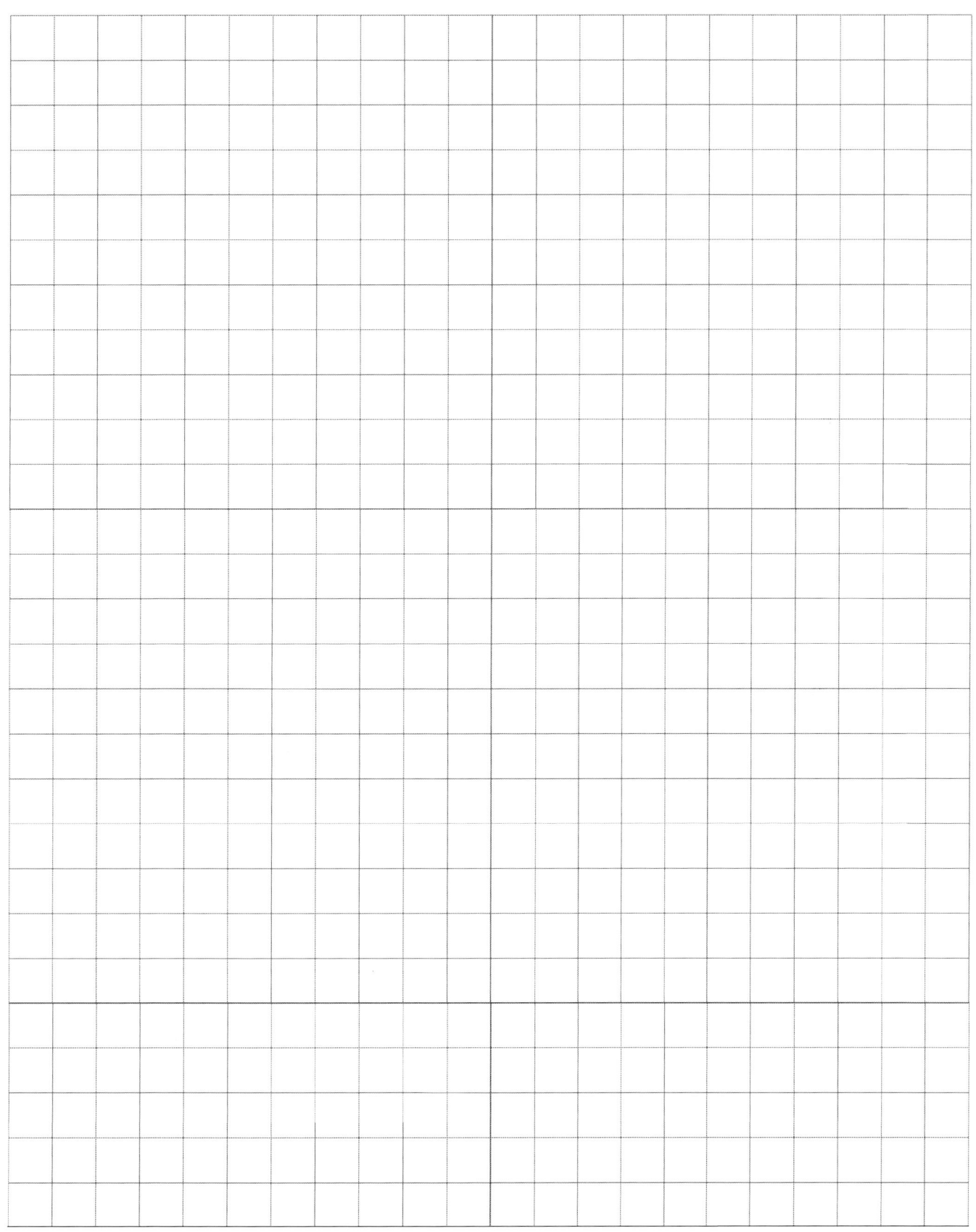

planner

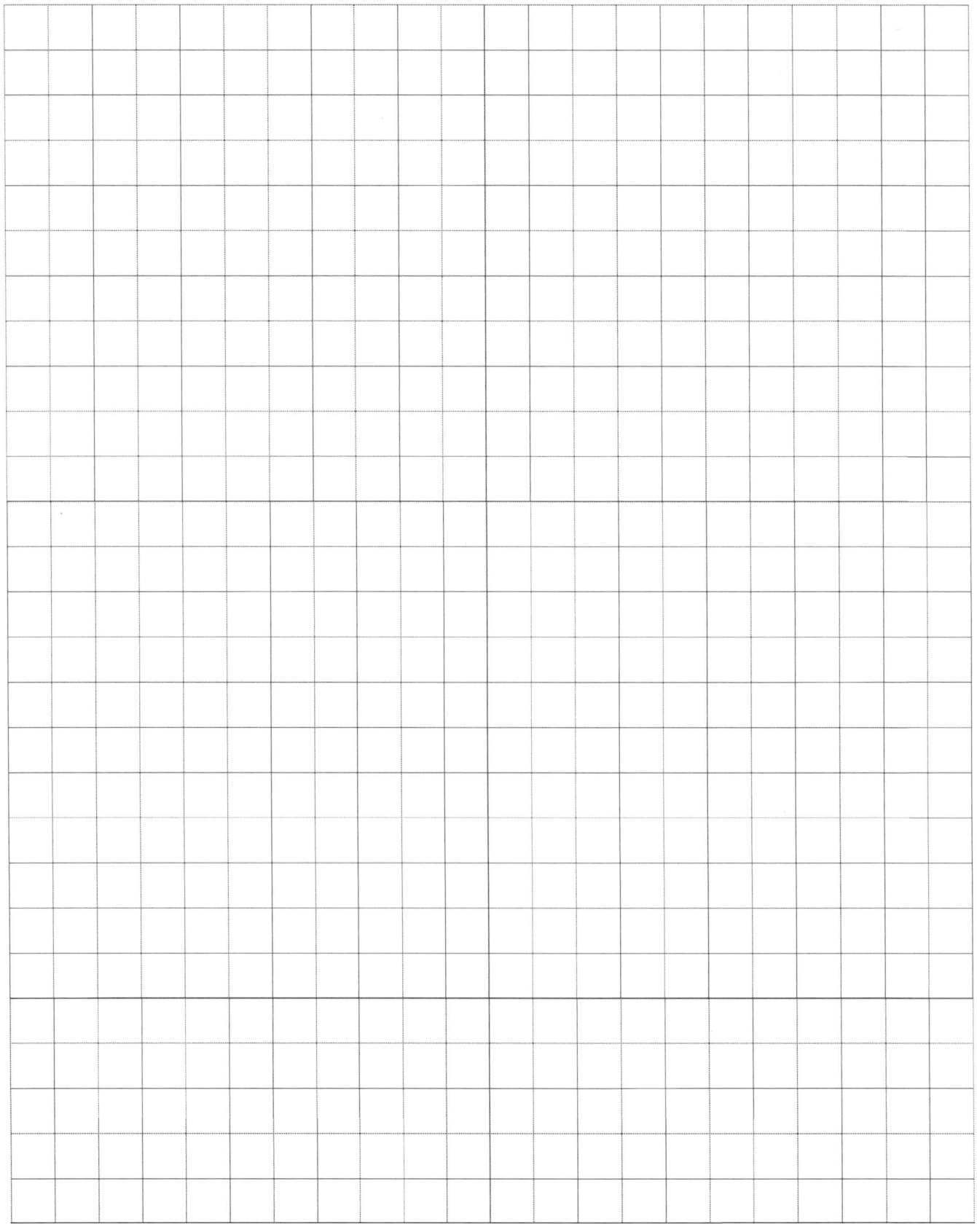

planner

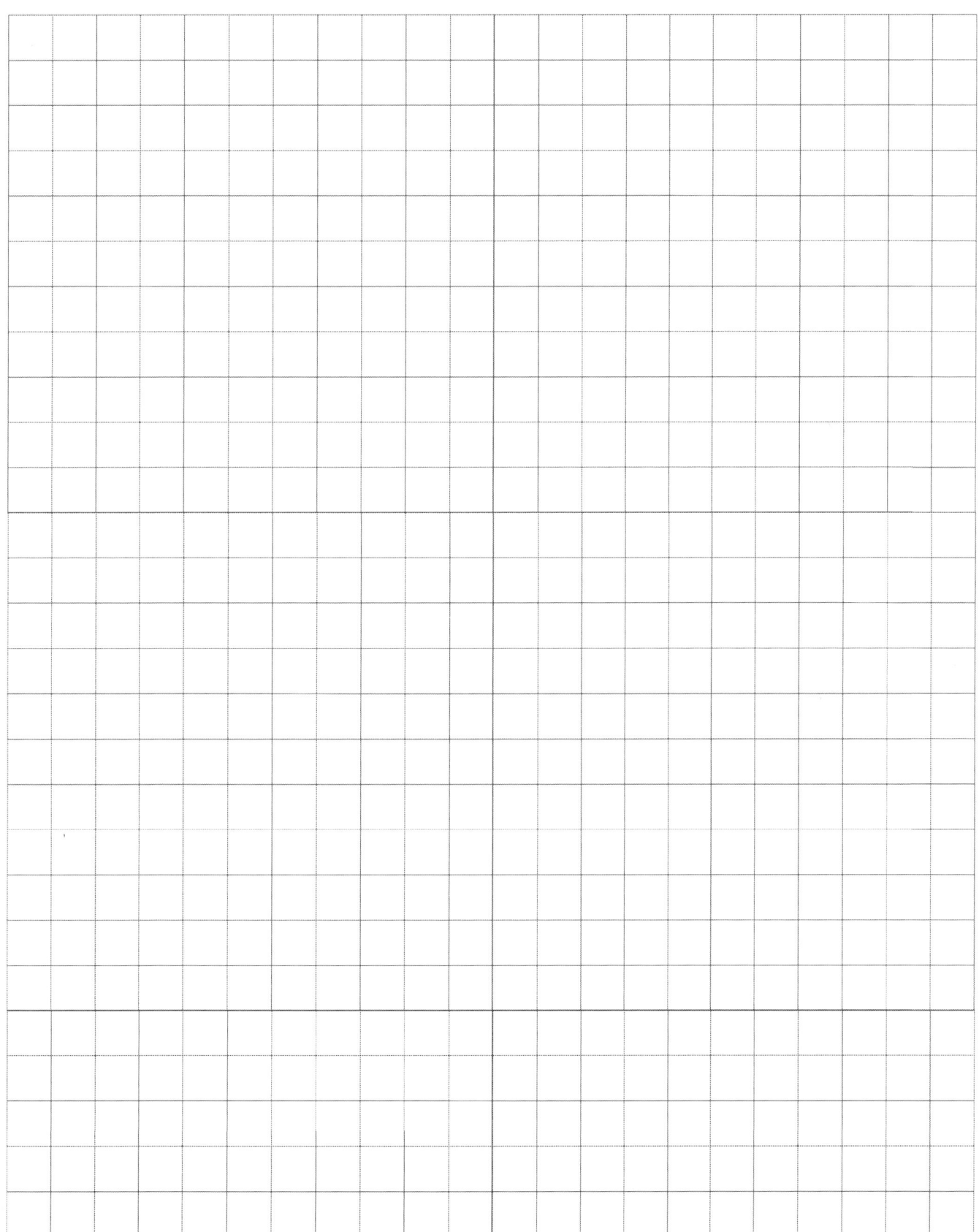

planner

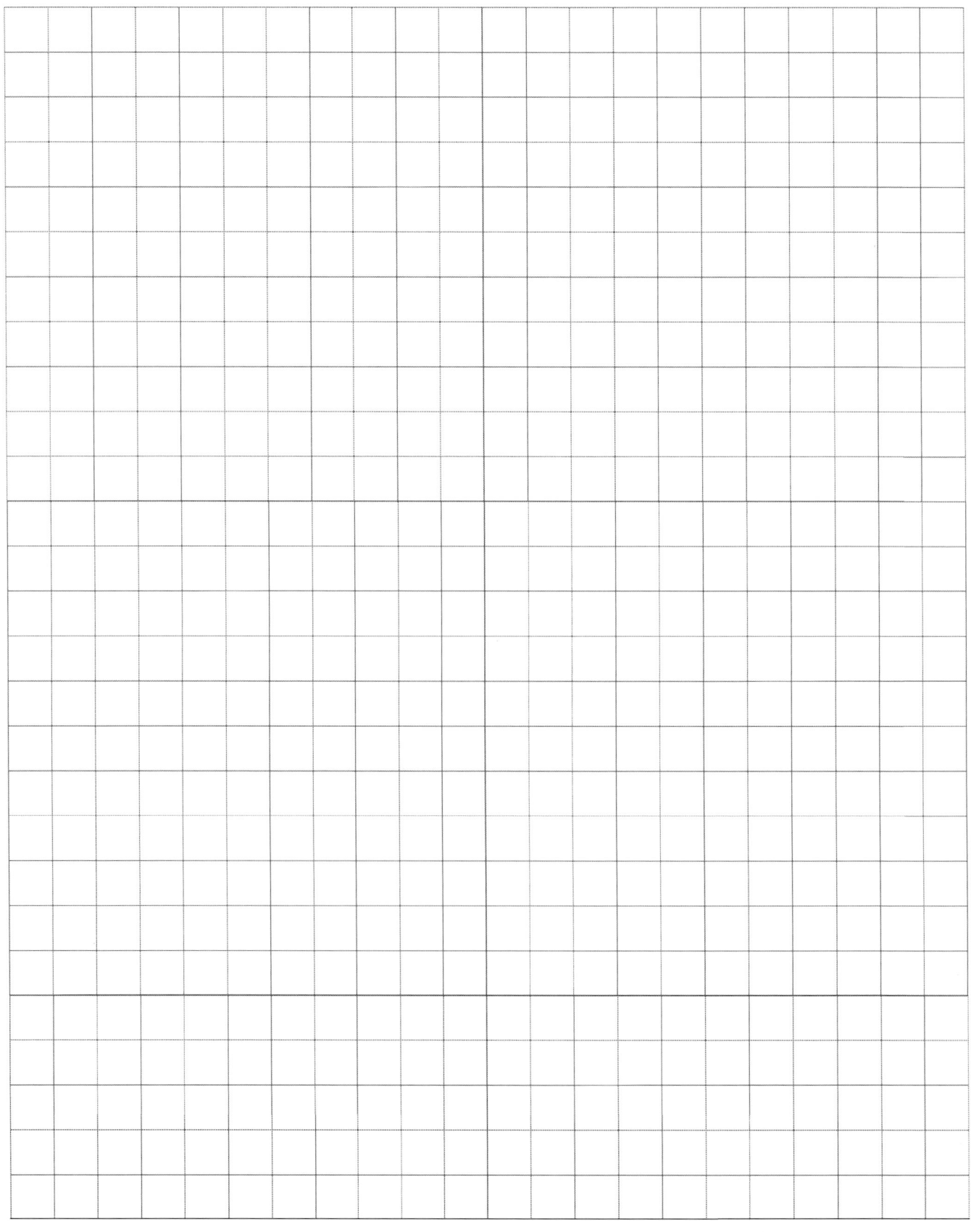

Made in the USA
Monee, IL
19 February 2024

488141a4-7e43-48e9-9223-39ed48678d4cR01